BORDER/BETWEEN:
A SYMPHONY IN ESSAYS

Carol D. Marsh

LOS ANGELES † NEW YORK † LONDON † MELBOURNE

Border/Between: A Symphony in Essays by Carol D. Marsh
ISBN: 978-1-947240-53-7
eISBN: 978-1-947240-54-4

Cover artwork by Dennis Callaci
Chapbook design and layout by Mark Givens

"Requiem for the Fall" was published in *River Teeth*, Spring/
Summer 2018

For information:
Bamboo Dart Press
chapbooks@bamboodartpress.com

Bamboo Dart Press 021

www.pelekinesis.com

www.bamboodartpress.com

www.shrimperrecords.com

TABLE OF CONTENTS

FIRST MOVEMENT:

SONATA

Introduction

It could have been magic or miracle, and I felt it viscerally as one feels transcendent lessons. At seventeen and recoiling from the tumult of the sixties and early seventies—Mỹ Lai and Viet Nam, Selma and the South, King and the Kennedys—I began rehearsing Haydn's *Mass in Time of War* with the Delaware All-State Choir. Conductor Carl Druba showed us the enthralling internal logic of music with its contiguous keys separate yet fluid, harmonies built upon mathematical truths, themes and motifs recurring in different tonalities and tempi yet all the while cohering. Haydn wrote this Mass in 1796 when Austria was fearing invasion after the French Revolution had embroiled most of Europe in war. Druba showed us disharmonious moments in the *Benedictus* and *Agnus Dei*, unusual in all of Haydn's compositions and only fleeting in this one, intruding as fear breaks through faith. Gloria E. Anzaldúa, poet and author, once said, "By writing I put order in the world, give it a handle so I can grasp it." I imagine Haydn in Eisenstadt at his piano, quill pen notating impending chaos and his own fearful hope for order.

Perhaps this is when music and death intertwined for me: music and sorrow, music and depths, emotions ineffable. Music and writing are this, handgrips on life and its seeming dichotomies: Haydn composing himself with a mass about war; Anzaldúa exploring and redefining borders as places in which, though we pretend it's not so, we live. Perhaps this is why I write most often of what causes me intense sorrow yet I cannot ignore. I write my disquiet, that which both repulses and draws me, gaining solace from examining the connective tissues between seeming opposites: violence and peace, sorrow and hope, living and dying. Humankind's unkindnesses.

Exposition

Gloria E. Anzaldúa was bitten by a snake when she was young. Forever afterward she identified with the Aztec goddess, Coatlicue, whose name means "snakes-her-skirt" and is always depicted wearing a garment of snakes. She birthed the moon and stars, says one version of her myth, after being beheaded by her own children who were enraged that she was pregnant. Coatlicue's face is comprised of two coiled serpents facing each other, representing blood—precious to Aztecs as symbolizing fertility—streaming from her severed neck. Stories about her are both terrifying and comforting. She's said to cause instability and fear, but also to protect women in childbirth, exemplifying the sorts of dualities Anzaldúa examined and deconstructed in her 1987 prose-poetry book, *Borderlands*. She strove to integrate three aspects of her identity as a queer, bi-lingual, Texan Chicana, having noted how Western cultures cleave body, mind, and spirit, and the inevitable chaos of the estrangement. Anzaldúa posited her own framework, or fourth culture: the body's relationship to and interaction with the divine. The intensity of this interplay, she said, creates a psychic knowledge that she came to see as her greatest strength, marginalized though it was by Westerners dismissing it as subjective. Embracing and living between the borders of what might be perceived as never to meet—Mexico and Texas, straight and queer, Spanish and English, subjective and objective—she discovered the identity she would claim and embrace as woman, poet, author, and intellectual.

Greek myth, in its own version of a double-serpent face, gives us the twins, Artemis and Apollo. Artemis is goddess of the hunt, of wildness and of animals, symbol of girlish beauty and chastity. Apollo is god of music and poetry, prophecy and healing of diseases, the personification of youthful beauty and nobility. Like Coatlicue, their myths are of violence and death yet also art and beauty. Always, it seems, our stories have coalesced around contradictions in our quest to put a handle to our world and, what's more needful, ourselves. Western culture's tragic mistake, under which Anzaldúa suffered but reconstructed as transformative insight, is refusing to embrace the liminal spaces between incongruities and dualities. Instead we hold to the opposites and in the process wrench apart body, mind and spirit— humanity's enactment of nuclear fission.

Development

My parents were both musical. Mom played piano for us and Dad loved to sing, leading his four kids in song during long car rides to our grandparents in Niagara Falls. One sweet and memorable trip home from college, my Dad and I sang Christmas carols. He took bass while I sang melody. Dad often told us about the seven-man octet in which he performed in college, and knowing his voice's resonance and carrying power, it made sense to us that the group's director decided there was no need for a second man on bass. He had Robert Marsh.

My grandmother used to predict we'd all grow up to be musicians. Her prediction didn't hold, as only my flautist sister went professional. But my brother played trombone and guitar, my other sister played piano and percussion, and I sang, each of us proficient enough to earn places in Delaware All-State and elite musical groups. Only singing could ease my near-chronic anxiety. Highly sensitive and acutely observant, I'd found in music and singing a way to manage my despair witnessing war, assassination, racism, and riotous violence. My brother once told me his trombone playing, especially while accompanying his *Chicago* albums, eased the incipient and undiagnosed OCD that would worsen from anxiety to full-blown mental illness in his twenties. This seemed our own problem, if not fault. Teen mental illness was not then an acceptable diagnosis, much less seen as deserving treatment. Now my brother's dead, and I think of his OCD as driving the alcohol addiction that killed him just before he turned 62. Addiction had made him unrecognizable— the conscientious, social boy become a morally compromised, distant man. I recognized aspects of my own war with codependence and people-pleasing, battles that seemed to me a matter of spiritual life and death, in the way alcohol divided Bill's principled spirit from his craven, needy body. It's unthinking, it's about nothing but naked need when addiction takes over. Death, in one form or another, is always the result. Family, having been murdered in its own way, is left to mourn.

Recapitulation

During my fifties I realized I held an unconscious, pessimistic and even apocalyptic expectation of human-kind's long-term viability and my own longevity. The expectation, shocking though it was when it surfaced to consciousness, had a flavor of inevitability about it. It wasn't that I'd been imagining eternal youth. I'd been expecting wholesale destruction, a cynicism that had become so ingrained I didn't know it was there to query. Hadn't I sat at fifteen, frozen with horror, watching a film about Hiroshima? When I learned Robert Oppen-heimer and his Los Alamos colleagues had named that bomb *Little Boy*, I wondered whether they had a macabre sense of humor, or, unconsciously troubled by what they were unleashing upon the world, couldn't proceed without minimizing its power and their respon-sibility. Like my brother pursuing the bottle to the detriment of all else, like me striving to please at the expense of my very self, humankind is so addicted to intellect or superiority that we can pursue knowledge up to and including the possibility of our own destruction. We are the children of Coatlicue, turning upon our own Mother and beheading her. We ignore the truth of the between, living at what we prefer to believe are incontrovertible borders. Pretending there's no middle ground and so creating whatever horror it contains, we disavow our agency. Unable and unwilling to see how our unconscious desires drive us, we cut off at the neck that which gives us life. We split mind, spirit and body, life and death, exploding our world.

Conclusion

As Haydn could envision his beloved country overtaken by Italian and Swiss troops yet create a *Kyrie* of surpassing sweetness, so can I undergird unthinkable mass destruction with prayerful hope. As Anzaldúa could make her home in the liminal space between knife-edged borders of language, culture, and sexuality, so can I describe addiction's destroying effects on families and on children and reject judgment, instead seeking compassion. I can write of death and, though broken, make it beautiful. Writing is this for me, the solace of interstitial spaces. I write, and it's subjective and truthful. I write, and reject the tyranny of absolutism.

I note where dissonance breaks through consonance and consonance reverberates through dissonance. I seek what lies between for this is where I feel welcome, and this is where I live.

SECOND MOVEMENT:

HUSH

Remember this: Crystal died twenty years ago.

Her death torments, haunts, and bedevils me. I know I'm choosing too many words. I choose too many to describe her life: entangled, ensnared, enmeshed. Ruined. Crystal's life was intertwined with the actions of a woman I never met and whose name I don't remember.

As Crystal lay dying, a song played in my head. A spiritual, "Hush." I'd never heard her sing it, but it underscored my last hours with her, sitting at her bedside in the small, neat room that was the first all her own and the last in her life. Those words and the tune—a pedal tone.

A pedal tone is a sustained note that doesn't change though the harmonies above it shift and flow. It's a webbing, it's what's between.

Or perhaps it was more like the reverberation of a

singing bowl, the small brass bowl I place on its multi-colored cushion, now, while I write Crystal into my heart. The cushion I cradle in my palm while I pick up the mallet. The mallet I gently place against and then run around the rim of the small brass bowl.

At first, I hear nothing. I hold the mallet firmly. I maintain its connection with the bowl. My hand circles, unwavering.

⋆   ⋆   ⋆

Hush, hush, somebody's callin' my name …
Oh my Lord, oh my Lord, what shall I do?

Remember this: Words like *haunts* and *bedevils* and *ensnared* and *entangled* spill from me when I write about Crystal, her life, her death, and the woman I never met whose name I don't remember.

The pedal tone of my Crystal memory is sorrow, yet there is, poised above it, a limpid melody.

The pedal tone of my woman memory (how can I have a memory of someone I never met?) is anger. Through it coils a discordant leitmotif: why did she do it?

What she did: she called a name.

I seek understanding: I imagine the woman.

On that day, I imagine she knows—perhaps it's a trembling of her fingers? a roiling in her gut?—agony is to come. An outlandish agony, not to be borne even in its mere anticipation. It destroys, as can nothing and no one, the stupor in which she exists and which, since the first needle prick drawing a drop of blood from her young forearm, has passed for peace. She has come otherwise to live not in the midst of life but on its panicked edges, craving this fickle repose. If there's an in-between, she hardly attends to it. For now, what brings her into the moment is nausea, trembling.

It's coming.

She calls a name, "Crystal!" An act that will reverberate throughout Crystal's life and death, malevolent.

Crystal is her daughter.

Do I blame the woman? Yes. There was a time I spat out her name. If you'd heard my voice when I said it, you'd have known I was capable of hate. Because on that day I try to imagine, she called her 12-year-old daughter's name for a purpose that all these years later still wrenches my heart into a bitter knot.

*　　*　　*

I must be patient with my singing bowl, serene in the gentle pressure fingers apply to mallet, faithful to circling hand. At first, I hear only a whisper of wood on brass. I must listen carefully or I'll miss the just-beyond-inaudible beginning.

*   *   *

I'm so glad trouble won't last always …
Oh, my Lord, oh my Lord, what shall I do?

Remember this: the woman who made the decision I'm trying to understand was Crystal's mother.

I met Crystal when she was twenty-four and moving into the home I ran for Washington D.C.'s women living with AIDS. She was 5'8" and 105 pounds with sunken, intense eyes in an emaciated face. She'd spent most of her life in survival mode on D.C. streets.

Aside from her death and the facts of her life, there are two things I remember about Crystal. One is the way she'd confront us in her tough-woman way, suggesting improvements in the community. The other is her joy.

"Why y'all ain't put a better ashtray on the smoker's patio? Them little things on the table are a mess. You should get one of the tall ones, you know, with sand in the bottom and a hole in the top for putting the cigarettes in." I see her proud smile when we bought the ashtray, put it on the patio, and I thanked her for the suggestion the next Tuesday during house meeting.

I see the way she'd wrap an arm around her best girlfriend and sweep out the front door, cash in her pocket and Checkers' burgers and shakes on her mind. Then, she was happy in a way that reminded me of my own more carefree teenage years. But that's where any similarity ended. Not only because I grew up in leafy suburbs, riding my bike on wide streets and playing in the creek, but more importantly, because the people who knew my name—my parents and other kids' parents, ministers and teachers—were trustworthy. When they called to me, it may not always have been positive (*Carol Daviss Marsh, get in here right now!*), but it was always safe.

One day Crystal's mother called her name and from that day Crystal was never safe again.

* * *

This is the beginning: I've stayed attentive to my singing bowl. At first, I sense it more than hear it. Not a sound so much as a vibration, what lies between note and no note.

*　　*　　*

Soon one morning, death come creepin' in my room ...
Oh my Lord, oh my Lord, what shall I do?

Remember this: that day her mother called her name, Crystal was twelve years old.

She was twelve years old.

I know about Crystal and her mother not because she told me, but from my staff members responsible for her admission. In our little community of women with harrowing stories they needed no longer—could no longer—keep hidden, Crystal was distinctive. She didn't talk about her early life, or how she'd contracted AIDS, or what her mother had done that day by calling her name. Not in the dining room after a meal, when other women shared stories about addiction, imprisonment, cruelty inflicted, mistakes made, and abuse endured. Not in the TV room during a Lifetime Channel movie that elicited memories of hard times. Not when others cursed those whose cruelty or neglect had irrevocably damaged their hopes. Crystal never joined in.

I didn't get to know her very well or even spend

much time with her until just after her 25th birthday. Not until her final illness forced her to bed did she want and accept my company. We'd watch television or listen to her gospel CDs. She'd ask for a foot massage, or help combing her pillow-mussed hair, or a dish of butter pecan ice cream. I'd dial the phone when her fingers were too weak to manage it herself, then hold the receiver to her ear so she could whisper an invitation to her mother. Later, she'd ask whether her mother had called back, and I'd speak a soft, sad negative. None of us, no one but Crystal, expected she'd get the calls or visits for which she so longed. We couldn't summon the will to say so, yet perhaps we too held out hope. At some level it was unthinkable, the possibility that a mother would not come to her terminally ill, pleading daughter.

And then, the long night of her dying.

This was a dying more struggle and hope than any other I'd attended. All the while, past the time of being able to speak, past the very act of breathing, Crystal's voiceless agitation called, or seemed to call, a name.

Whose name should be called out on a death bed? Someone beloved, someone loving. A spouse or partner, a parent, child, or sibling. Darling grandbaby. Jesus, maybe. Or Allah. Jehovah. God and the angels.

What if the name called out were that of the mother who had, when her daughter (now dying) was a skinny 12-year-old, said her name and then handed her over to the man standing there with money in his hand and lust in his eyes? Should final hours be consumed with grabbing the empty air, eyes darting, staring, for this mother who prostituted her daughter (now dying) because she needed money to pay for the drugs that would stop, stop, *stop* her agony?

Does that mother deserve her daughter's love and longing, not her condemnation and hate?

Yet this is how Crystal died.

This is how she died.

I held Crystal and whispered we loved her and how beautiful she was, hoping for peace and a home not granted her in this world. Crystal grasped and gasped and died, and I remember sitting, low, on her bed, holding her and I remember her jaw opening and closing, opening and closing, and she was not breathing but unceasing was the reverberation of her longing for her pimp of a mother.

The pedal tone of Crystal's death is forgiveness.

Sounds like Jesus, Jesus callin' my name …
Oh my Lord, oh my Lord, what shall I do?

Remember this: she was twelve years old when her mother called her name that day.

She was twelve years old.

Do I seem bitter? Well, I am.

Yet.

*　　*　　*

The tone emanating from the bowl is at first faint, so faint. I'm entranced, my circling hand, unfaltering. I listen.

*　　*　　*

Hush, hush, somebody's callin' my name ...
Oh my Lord, oh my Lord, what shall I do?

Remember this: I never knew the woman.

What had happened to Crystal's mother that she could do such a thing? When she was young, who had called her name and for what purpose? Something sounds within me.

I seek to understand: I imagine her.

Her fingers trembling, she opens her mouth to call. Even through the ragged scrim of gathering withdrawal, the degradation—the irredeemable shame—of what she's about to do courses through her. All of it, all her life's experiences and circumstances and decisions have come to this and it's so much worse than she ever could have imagined. So much worse as to make her compulsion more insistent and her shame more horrifying, as to make relief that much more necessary. Awash in the maelstrom sucking her down and down and down, she calls a name. This name, though it obtains for her momentary bliss, can only ever temporarily stave off agony. This name and the fleeting release it purchases can only ever engulf her in guilt.

I imagine this is why she wasn't home the day we took an emaciated Crystal—hopeful at first, then increasingly distraught, then silent—for a pre-arranged final visit, after which Crystal slumped into the bed in which she remained until death came a week later. Perhaps it was why she never came to her dying daughter, never responded to all our imploring phone messages, did not appear at Crystal's funeral.

The pedal tone of the woman's life is shame.

*　　*　　*

The ringing is low at first and quite faint. My hand circles. A gradual crescendo enfolds an internal, sonorous pulse. There is, in motion and tonality and rhythm, that which calms. It stills my breath and slows my heart and quiets my thoughts. My hand circles. A groundswell, timbre pure and bright. To hear it I must remain faithful to mallet on bowl, to steady circling hand, to the gentle, firm, continuous pressure of fingers on wood and wood on brass.

I desire compassion as the pedal tone of my life so I allow the resonance its way. I permit an untethering of hatred, judgment and opinion, allowing a softening of sharp edges.

I listen.

Hush.

The bowl sings.

THIRD MOVEMENT:

SONG FOR THE DYING

Intro

He's awake. It's night, late night, and he's restless in the hospital bed. Reaching for his phone, he fumbles around the table among a mess of unopened cracker packets, used napkins, empty cups, and a bowl of watery, warm Jell-O still tightly covered with plastic wrap. Hoping for relief from pain and despair, or perhaps only seeking distraction, he chooses a song.

Verse One

The opening notes startle me, this song's title having led me to expect something quieter, more reflective. A descending slash of a single string on Eric Clapton's electric guitar is immediately pounced upon by drums and bass for the downbeat. It's urgent, loud, and gets more so with the entrance of the brass section: producer Phil Spector's signature "wall of sound." By the time George Harrison enters on vocals, I'm bemused. Circumstances have set me up for another song altogether.

George's voice is pressing, yet gentle, over the insistent instruments. His phrasing is smooth. He's not shouting. George rarely shouts. He's simply there, with them all, responding to the moment Eric propels them, irresistibly, into this song.

It's "The Art of Dying," from Harrison's 1970 album, *All Things Must Pass*.

Pre-Chorus

My brother, Bill, loved music, jazz especially. He played trombone and guitar, accompanying his albums, learning the harmonies and persisting until his arms grew too tired to hold the instrument.

Chorus

Once we were best friends, Bill and me. In the sixties we were children together, and he'd teach me football plays or how to pitch side-arm. He'd slip notes printed in his cramped hand under my bedroom door, maybe about a concert we'd attended or a swim meet in which I'd competed. Later, much later, when we were older and he was drinking and we were no longer best friends, and though he'd often neglect to answer my messages, he'd still send me links to songs. He'd note a guitar riff he loved or something in the lyrics: music as connective tissue, the fascia of our adult siblinghood.

Verse Two

It begins with two fleeting guitar notes pushing to the downbeat. Fleeting, yet essential. They've indicated tempo and key and brought the other instruments in. As I listen to this version of "The Art of Dying"—Joel Harrison's jazz cover, the one I believe Bill favored— I imagine Joel playing those notes while the other musicians wait, poised and alert.

The beginning phrases repeat and they're all playing now, keyboard, bass, drums, and Joel on guitar and vocals. With volume at mezzo forte, the tempo drives ahead, though not quite as fast as George's original. This instrumentation is no wall of sound. It's spare, open. A window.

Joel's voice—a bit harsher, less melodically pleasant than George's—better fits the lyrics. Would I have thought so had I heard the song before? Maybe. To me, listening for the first time after Bill's fiancé tells me it's on his playlist, Joel sounds as though he suffers the roughened throat of one holding back tears. His phrases are not smooth and sustained, but broken.

Verse Three

Bill, at sixty-one years old, weighed about 300 pounds. He had chronic obstructive pulmonary disease (COPD), diabetes, herniated discs, an infected heart valve—the replacement valve from surgery a decade before—and a deteriorating liver and pancreas. The diabetes was caused, he said, by the steroids managing his COPD. But surely all the drinking didn't help.

The last time I saw him he was in week seven of what would become a nine-week hospitalization. He'd gone through detox at the beginning. I knew, from his descriptions of other detoxes, it must have been agony. He didn't mention it. During that visit Bill was looking to the future. He'd talked about making changes. He'd stop drinking. Stop chasing money. Get rid of some other bad habits. He'd allow his business to continue its slide into bankruptcy. Stop fighting what he couldn't change and didn't want any longer anyway.

He'd described a scene from a movie he'd watched some years before and couldn't forget. "I want to live like that," I remember him saying, "in a community with friends and family, sharing music. Being together. A simpler life." I heard a wistful quality, or think I remember hearing a wistful quality, in his voice. Am I imagining it because I know now what I didn't know then? I don't know. Maybe I'm directing the scene as I need it to be, not as it was. Because of all the thousands of hours of movies he'd watched over his lifetime, this single scene is the one upon which he dwelt when I last saw him.

He died of a massive stroke two weeks later.

Pre-Chorus

Bill never sent me "The Art of Dying." No, that's not why I write about it now.

Chorus

Once we were best friends, Bill and me. In the sixties we were children together, and he'd teach me football plays or how to pitch side-arm. He'd slip notes printed in his cramped hand under my bedroom door, maybe about a concert we'd attended or a swim meet in which I'd competed. Later, much later, when we were older and he was drinking and we were no longer best friends, and though he'd often neglect to answer my messages, he'd still send me links to songs. He'd note a guitar riff he loved or something in the lyrics: music as connective tissue, the fascia of our adult siblinghood.

Verse Four

It was eighteen months before I felt able to find and stream the movie Bill had talked about. I hesitated before locating the scene, its significance a weight I needed to be certain I could shoulder. Finally, I steeled myself to begin scanning for what he'd described.

A huge bonfire backlights figures throwing tree branches into the blaze at one hour, forty-one minutes and fifty seconds into Sean Penn's *Into the Wild*. The scene lasts exactly one minute: it's evening in California's Slab City, the Sonoran Desert RV community built, by snow-birders seeking a place to overwinter, upon the concrete foundations of a former military base. The camera scans a crowd of people alit in lambent flames, all standing and facing a large stage. Some are arm in arm. Some, tending to children. A long, draping cord of outdoor lights frames the stage from above, a proscenium of sorts. A young man and woman perform, he on keyboard, she on guitar and vocals: "Angel from Montgomery," by John Prine. What's being sung, in this setting of gloaming and fire and desert and gathered peoples, holds an unbearable poignancy. Because this, too, is a song my brother sent me. Not by email but in story.

Prine was intrigued by the idea of "a song about a middle-aged woman who feels older than she is ... [Eventually] I had this really vivid picture of this woman standing over the dishwater with soap in her hands. ... She wanted to get out of her house and her marriage and everything. She just wanted an angel to come to take her away from all this." She believed that only in being taken from all she has and knows will she find something to hold onto.

A vision to hold onto, maybe: a fire, a community gathered, a desert night. Music.

Verse Five

When my grief is not too raw for solace, I return to "The Art of Dying." I hear it as though for the first time, wondering at sorrow's iron and somewhat capricious grip. More than the bonfire scene, this song—Joel Harrison's jazz version—grieves me.

It grieves me because I'd heard Bill's wishes for the life he never got to live. And because I'd never seen him again. And because it's the song he chose on his final night. The song he never sent me is the one I hear and see as though there with him when he seeks comfort in the troubled dark.

Bridge

George Harrison recorded "The Art of Dying" in 1970, though he'd begun writing it as early as 1966. He'd started the lyrics after his first LSD trip, during which he heard a whisper, *yogis of the Himalaya.* Thus, feeling invited into a spirituality in which he'd sojourn for the rest of his life, he wrote about reincarnation in this song as well as in "Give Me Love (Give Me Peace on Earth)." Phrases in "The Art of Dying" seem to acknowledge, in a sly or humorous way, skepticism or disbelief on the part of his audience. He asks us if we're still with him, whether we believe him.

Maybe it's not slyness. Maybe it's the sort of question we whisper to death, to the dead. *Are you still with me?*

Chorus

Once we were best friends, you and me. In the sixties we were children together, and you'd teach me football plays or how to pitch side-arm. You'd slip notes printed in your cramped hand under my bedroom door, maybe about a concert we'd attended or a swim meet in which I'd competed. Later, much later, when we were older and you were drinking and we were no longer best friends, and though you'd often neglect to answer my messages, you'd still send me links to songs. You'd note a guitar riff you loved or something in the lyrics: music as connective tissue, the fascia of our adult siblinghood.

Outro

You're awake. It's night, late night, and you're restless in the hospital bed. You reach for your phone, fumbling around the table among a mess of unopened cracker packets, used napkins, empty cups, and a bowl of watery, warm Jell-O still tightly covered with plastic wrap. Hoping for relief from pain and despair, or perhaps only seeking distraction, you choose what your playlist shows is the last song you ever heard and what is now the fascia of my grief and your death: Joel Harrison's cover of "The Art of Dying."

Are you still with me?

FOURTH MOVEMENT:

REQUIEM FOR THE FALL

If I were a composer, I'd create a Requiem Mass and entitle it, *Requiem for the Fall*.

I'd compose *Requiem for the Fall* because I want not to forget.

I want not to forget because I believe in prayers for mercy.

∴   ∴   ∴

Requiem is a funeral Mass, from the Latin, *Missa pro defunctis*, "Mass for the dead." Since high school, I've sung soprano in Requiems composed by Joseph Haydn, Wolfgang Amadeus Mozart, Giuseppi Verdi, Johannes Brahms, John Rutter and Gabriel Faure, often wailing as much as singing, my throat a living passage for the hopeful, angry, frightened, beseeching grief that is the voice of those left behind.

A Requiem typically begins with the *Introit*, which sets the tonality of the piece and often indicates themes to come.

∴

These are the colors of a candle flame: blue at the bottom; orangey-brown in the middle; yellow from there to the top of the flame, just below where grey smoke lifts and curls.

∴

These are the colors of an atom bomb: white; then yellow; then orange-red that becomes violet. Finally, the grey mushroom cloud rising, enormous.

∴

These are the colors of a documentary I saw about Hiroshima in 1972 when I was seventeen: black and white and grey.

∴   ∴   ∴

Originally written in Latin—the language of the Catholic Church until the mid-1960s—the Mass was chanted by the priest. Later, composers used the structure, words, and settings and set them to music. For centuries, composers stayed with Latin. More recently, Requiems have been written in English: Rutter's, for example. Brahms' is in German.

∴

I was once a teenager who learned about the bombing of Hiroshima and then went home to dinner. Before we ate, my mother, in a longtime tradition, lit a candle. A taper in a bottle. The six of us, four kids seated on the longer sides of the rectangular wood table, my parents opposite each other at the ends, in the blue kitchen with my sister's framed embroidery on the wall: *No matter where I serve my guests, it seems they like my kitchen best.* We called them romantic drippings, the wax flowing warmly down the bottle before cooling into formations simultaneously random and gentle.

∴

Robert Oppenheimer named the first atom bomb test-site Trinity, though later he couldn't recall why. The men—scientists who'd lived and worked at Los Alamos building the world's latest and most efficient weapon of mass destruction—assembled in the New Mexico desert twenty miles away from Trinity on an early morning in July 1945. Martin J. Sherwin and Kai Bird describe the scene in *American Prometheus: The Triumph and Tragedy of Robert Oppenheimer*: "All of a sudden, the night turned into day and it was tremendously bright, the chill turned into warmth; the fireball gradually turned from white to yellow to red as it grew in size and climbed into the sky; after about five seconds the darkness returned but with the sky and the air filled with a purple glow, just as though we were surrounded by an aurora borealis." Then, an "unearthly hovering cloud."

∴

I watched the Hiroshima documentary in my high school social studies class, sitting in one of the martial rows of student desks facing the front of the room and the teacher's desk. Seeing the film gave me a stiff neck, though whether that was because I had to turn my head to watch the screen set up in the right-front corner of the classroom or because I had frozen with horror, I don't know.

∴   ∴   ∴

Though composers often choose to omit sections and reprise certain phrases, the structure of the Requiem Mass is fixed: the *Introit*, then the *Kyrie*, then the *Dies irae*. Then the *Offertorium, Sanctus, Benedictus, Agnus*

Dei, Lux Aeterna, and *Libera Me.* Verdi followed this structure – that of the Latin Requiem Mass—exactly, while Faure omitted whole sections and Brahms threw in a section or two of his own invention.

∴

My parents had precise and detailed instructions about manners. Elbows off the table. Don't talk with food in your mouth. Sit up straight. Chew with your mouth closed. If you can't say something nice, don't say anything at all. Cut your meat with the knife in your right hand and your fork in your left hand. When you're finished eating, place your utensils at 4:00 on your plate. It was pleasing, this imposed order, to my harmony-loving self.

∴

Oppenheimer gave exacting instructions for delivering the weapon, which he called "the gadget," on target and to inflict maximum damage. They were not to drop it on a rainy or foggy day, nor through clouds. It had to be a visual drop, no radar. If at night, there must be a moon bright enough for good visibility. And the gadget mustn't detonate at too high an altitude. "Don't let it go up [higher] or the target won't get as much damage," he said.

∴

Throughout World War II, American planes typically dropped leaflets over soon-to-be-bombed cities, instructing the people to evacuate and/or put pressure on their leaders to surrender. An enduring myth of Hiroshima, and one that Americans still use to justify bombing that city and Nagasaki, is that the citizens were warned beforehand. But they weren't. Powerful American men decided not to drop leaflets warning the inhabitants of their impending, unimaginable destruction. They feared the Japanese military, forewarned, would shoot the bomber down.

∴   ∴   ∴

The *Kyrie* movement of a musical setting of the *Missa pro defunctis* is in three parts, essentially expressing the Trinity—Creator, Redeemer, Sanctifier—in structure: *Kyrie eleison, Christe eleison, Kyrie eleison.*

▷ Lord have mercy,
▷ Christ have mercy,
▷ Lord have mercy.

The text of the Agnus Dei (*Lamb of God*):

- ▷ Lamb of God, who takes away the sins of the world, have mercy upon us.
- ▷ Lamb of God, who takes away the sins of the world, have mercy upon us.
- ▷ Lamb of God, who takes away the sins of the word, grant us peace.

Composers use repetition and alternation of themes and motifs to bring this three-fold expression into the music. An example of this is the ternary form, ABA—where A represents a theme that is then succeeded by the B theme, followed by a repetition, sometimes with variations, of the A theme. And the ternary form is often amplified by a nine-fold structure, AAABBBCCC: three different themes, each repeated three times before the next begins. Themes can vary from one another in melody, harmony, and tonal center, but are always complementary in that they make musical sense together.

∴

Candle wax is essentially made of hydrocarbons. When heated by the flame, they break down into their component atoms—hydrogen and carbon:

- ▷ The atoms are vaporized.

- The vaporized atoms are pulled up into the candle flame.
- They react to the air's oxygen to create heat, light, water vapor and carbon dioxide.

That's how a candle flame works: vaporized atoms of hydrogen and carbon turn into heat, light, water vapor and carbon dioxide, all of which are released into the air. Thus the colors: blue at the bottom in the zone rich with oxygen; brown where hardened bits of carbon form—the leftovers of oxygen consumption; then yellow to the top of the flame.

∴

The core of the Hiroshima nuclear bomb, inside its metal encasement, is essentially a mass of uranium isotope U-235. A gun-type assembly method causes detonation, during which the isotope's nuclei are split. This produces highly charged neutrons and the immense energy of a chain reaction. That's why the bombs first tested in New Mexico and dropped on Hiroshima are called atom bombs or neutron bombs. In this splitting process, called fission:

- Detonation causes the splitting of one isotope nuclei, which releases highly charged (also called high-speed and radioactive) neutrons.

▹ These neutrons produced by the initial splitting strike nearby nuclei and produce more fission that becomes a self-sustaining process instantaneously producing radioactive energy.

▹ Impossible to contain, the radiation, heat, sound waves and light are released into the air.

Thus the colors: obliterating white in that first explosive instant, when atoms slam into atoms and break down isotopes. After the fireball, yellowish- or reddish-brown, due to the presence of nitrogen dioxide and nitric acid. Then, amid flashes of lightning, the cloud turns grey-white as water and ice condense out while the fireball cools. Finally, dark grey when smoke and debris are sucked into the updraft.

The Hiroshima bomb was named "Little Boy."

∴

A black-and-white documentary such as would have been shown to a high school class in 1972 is essentially a strip of plastic film coated with a single layer of gelatin emulsion. In the emulsion are suspended tiny, light-sensitive, silver halide crystals. These crystals absorb light when the film is momentarily exposed through a camera shutter, causing a change in the chemical make-up of the emulsion. Shades of black, white, and grey in the visible photo correspond to the amount of light absorbed by each microscopic silver halide crystal. Thus the colors of a black-and-white film about Hiroshima: dark, light, and shades of grey.

▷ The atom bomb cloud: white and grey.

▷ The destroyed city, the shadows of people incinerated in the act of casting wondering glances to the sky, the umbrae of buildings now mausoleums for vaporized lives: dark and grey.

▷ The survivors, tiny and slender, the sick ones in bed and the ones with skin sloughing away, the ones with their eyes carved out by what was seen and not seen: shades of grey.

One of the Little Boy survivors was named Tomiko Moromito.

∴   ∴   ∴

The third section of the Requiem—after the *Introit* and the *Kyrie*—is the *Dies irae*, "Day of Wrath." The first two lines: "The day of wrath, that dreadful day will dissolve the world in ashes." Musically, the *Dies irae* is often loud, a drumming, driving force. Mozart's sounds as though he wrote it expecting the Avenging God to come crashing through his window at any moment. Its tempo is fast, the strings insistent, and the choir's first words declaim each syllable of the opening phrase one by one, in almost martial cadence. Verdi's begins abruptly, forte, a staccato slash of strings echoed in a crash of tympani, repeated three more times before the choir enters on a rising phrase that stays, high and loud, on the first syllable of "irae" while strings and percussion swirl chaotically toward a repeat. One sings these movements with pounding heart.

∴

From *Voice of America*, "Hiroshima Survivor Recalls Day Atomic Bomb Was Dropped" (October 30, 2009): "Everything started falling down; all the buildings started flying around all over the place. Then something wet started coming down, like rain. I guess that's what they call black rain. In my child's mind, I thought it was oil. I thought the Americans were going to burn us to death. And we kept running. And fire was coming out right behind us, you know."

∴

After they'd pulled together their jangled senses and understood what had occurred, Sherwin and Bird wrote, the scientists witnessing the Trinity test yelled and shouted and danced at its stupendous success. They grasped one another's hands, jubilant, bathed in a warm breeze upon which wafted an invisible cloud of radio-active isotopes. One of the scientists at Trinity watched Oppenheimer that day and said later, "I'll never forget his walk … like High Noon, this kind of strut. He had done it."

∴

We sat together, night after night, as the candle shortened and its wax dripped. The six of us, always at the same place at the kitchen table, each with our cloth napkin and personal napkin ring. Mine was green. In the middle of the table, the walnut Lazy Susan. On its revolving surface, a sugar bowl, salt and pepper shakers, the bottle with its drippings. In the bottle, the red or blue or green or white candle, its black wick curling over pooled wax in the concave shelter of its base.

∴   ∴   ∴

The *Dies irae* ends with the *Pie Jesu*, "Merciful Jesus, grant them peace. Amen." Faure, whose Requiem's melodies and orchestration are replete with quiet suppli-cation and comfort—very different from the operatic grandeur of the Verdi—omitted the terrifying *Dies irea* altogether. Instead, he opted to set only the text of the

Pie Jesu, doing so with a contemplative, melodically simple soprano solo.

∴

Having lit the taper, helped my father serve the food, and settled into her chair, my mother would pick up her fork. This was the signal that we could all start eating.

∴

Having opened the bay doors and let Little Boy fall, the pilot, bombardier and navigator on the plane named Enola Gay after the pilot's mother, placed dark shields over their eyes in order not to be blinded by detonation. Once it was safe, they pulled off the blindfolds and looked back.

∴

Having survived the first detonation of an atomic bomb as an act of war, the ones who lived earned a special designation: *hibakusha*. It means "explosion-affected people." Motoko Rich, reporting for the *New York Times*, wrote of one *hibakusha* who was 20 years old and on his way to classes at the university. He survived the blast but was so badly burned and in such severe pain he was sure he was dying. He collapsed on a bridge, took a small rock and etched in stone, "Here is where Sunao Tsuboi found his end."

∴   ∴   ∴

The *Lacrymosa,* "day of weeping," occurs within the *Dies irae.* The sobbing violin motif that begins Mozart's *Lacrymosa* is taken up and embellished by the choir: an upward sweep on the syllable "*la*" that merely touches a higher note before descending quickly through "*cry*" to linger on the syllable "*mo*." Then a grieving, step-wise resolution to "*sa*." As close to simultaneously weeping and singing as I have ever come.

∴

This is what my high school mind couldn't fathom: Americans had killed an entire city with one bomb. They knew exactly what would happen but

▹ They dropped it anyway.
▹ They dropped it anyway.
▹ They dropped it anyway.

∴

This is what Robert Oppenheimer said when he was told his gadget had been let go over Hiroshima on

August 6, 1945, at 8:16 a.m., Japanese time: "Those poor people. Those poor little people."

∴

This is what *habukisha* Tomiko Morimoto said: "I go out the first thing in the morning and look at the sky and the sun and I am very appreciative of everything I have right now."

∴ ∴ ∴

A Requiem Mass ends with a prayer for liberation, the *Libera Me.* But I'd end my requiem with the *Agnus Dei,* "Lamb of God."

∴

I think my face, my seventeen-year-old-face, may have looked like this after I watched the Hiroshima documentary: older, greyer. I'd viewed it after formative years of agonized witness to assassinations and police wielding fire hoses and body bags delivered from Viet Nam that had caused me to question the very idea of a Christian God. It dealt one more in a long series of severe blows to my faith. My spirit eventually rejected the dogmatic rigidity of formal religion and found its peace in broader, more connective, places. Yet the structure and music of the Requiem Mass, for all its declamation of Catholic belief, pleases me and has never lost its power over me as a needful expression of grief for the suffering humankind brings to this world.

Lamb of God, who takes away the sins of the world, have mercy upon us.

I imagine an atom bomb looks like this having fallen through the transcendent perfection of a cloudless sky to its moment of detonation: monumental and devastating and timeless. When you're its target and you're watching the fall, it's the last thing you'll ever see. You will not witness the holocaust on the ground because you will have died before experiencing any gorgeous colors or lightning flashes. Before the psychedelic mushroom nudges the heavens, you will be ashes. No, not so substantial as ashes. Shadows. You and all nearby you will be shadows as soon as the sky explodes.

Lamb of God, who takes away the sins of the world, have mercy upon us.

A candle flame looks like this falling through its own base: subtle and spectacular and instantaneous. You must pay close attention to witness this falling. The flame, released from mooring of wick and wax, drops to the bottom of the bottle and you watch it fall through the gone romance of green glass. It drops and flares, briefly, as though in its demise are the seeds of its greatest power. The interior of the bottle is brilliantly alight, a nanosecond of purity. You watch unblinking and unbreathing in order not to miss it. You see the tiny fireball and, for that one flaring second, are blind to all else. From the darkness, a plume of smoke arises, a long, feathery dissipation into the air. You have held your breath anticipating this small moment that holds a woeful beauty for you. And so you exhale and shudder. Because you are a teenager who once watched a documentary about Hiroshima and then went home to dinner, you shudder.

Lamb of God, who takes away the sins of the world, grant us peace.

ABOUT THE AUTHOR

Carol D. Marsh earned her MFA in Nonfiction from Goucher College in 2014. Since then, her writing has won awards from National Indie Book Awards 2017, Sarton Women's Book Contest 2018, New Millennium Writings 2016, Under the Gum Tree 2018, Solstice Literary Magazine 2020, and Tucson Festival of Books 2021. Her essays have been published in *The Vassar Review, Chautauqua Journal, LA Review Best of the Year 2018,* and *River Teeth*, among others. She's currently working on a researched memoir about being a highly sensitive person (HSP), in which she weaves stories of her life with science, neurology, genetics, and interviews of a diverse cohort of other HSPs. Visit her website: carol@caroldmarsh.com.

112 N. Harvard Ave. #65
Claremont, CA 91711
chapbooks@bamboodartpress.com
www.bamboodartpress.com

CPSIA information can be obtained
at www.ICGtesting.com
Printed in the USA
JSHW051401160622
27127JS00003B/62